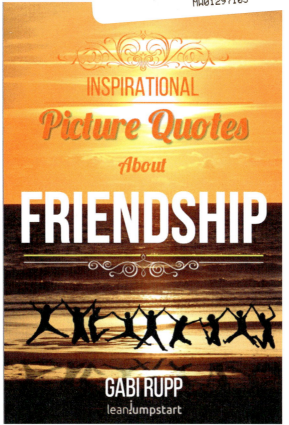

To:

From

Copyright © 2015 by **Gabi Rupp**

DISCLAIMER: This book contains material protected under International and Federal Copyright Laws and Treaties. Any unauthorized reprint or use of this material is prohibited. No part of this book may be reproduced or transmitted in any form or by any means, electronic or mechanical, including photocopying, recording, or by any information storage and retrieval system without express written permission from the publisher.

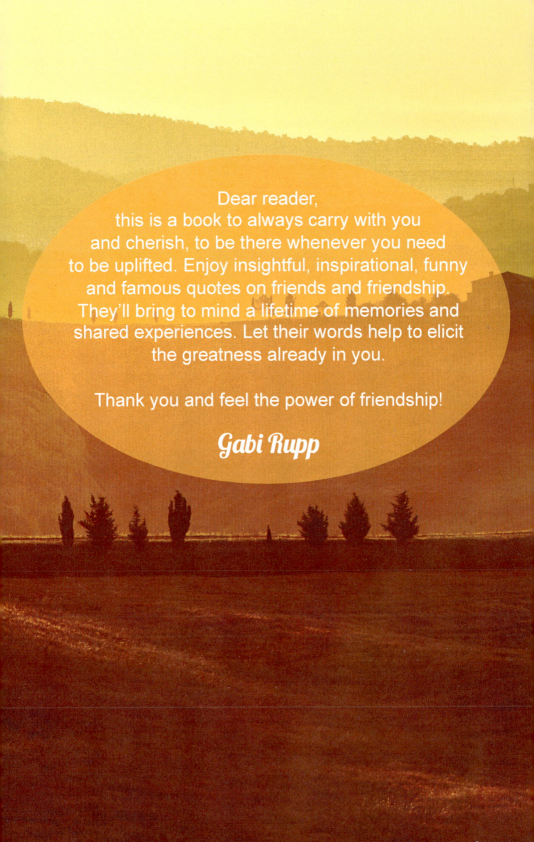

Dear reader,
this is a book to always carry with you and cherish, to be there whenever you need to be uplifted. Enjoy insightful, inspirational, funny and famous quotes on friends and friendship. They'll bring to mind a lifetime of memories and shared experiences. Let their words help to elicit the greatness already in you.

Thank you and feel the power of friendship!

Gabi Rupp

Attention

Be slow to fall into friendship, but when thou art in, continue firm and constant.
~Derek Bethune

If a man does not make new acquaintances as he advances through life, he will soon find himself alone. A man should keep his friendships in constant repair.
~Samuel Johnson

Men kick friendship around like a football, but it doesn't seem to crack. Women treat it like glass and it goes to pieces
~Anne Spencer Morrow Lindbergh

Friendships begin because, even without words, we **UNDERSTAND** *how someone feels.*

JOAN WALSH ANGLUND

> Friendship is born at that moment when one person says to another: What! You too? I thought I was the only one.
> ~C. S. Lewis

> One of the most beautiful qualities of true friendship is to understand and to be understood.
> ~Lucius Annaeus Seneca

> Friendship is a living thing that lasts only as long as it is nourished with kindness, empathy and understanding.
> ~Unknown

Compassion

IT TAKES A LONG TIME
to grow an old friend

JOHN LEONARD

Slow Growth

Though friendship
is not quick to burn,
it is explosive stuff.
~May Sarton

Be slow
in choosing a friend,
slower in changing.
~Benjamin Franklin

Wishing
to be friends
is quick work,
but friendship is
slow-ripening fruit.
~Aristotle

True friendship is
a plant of slow growth,
and must undergo
the shocks of adversity
before it is entitled
to the appellation.
~George Washington

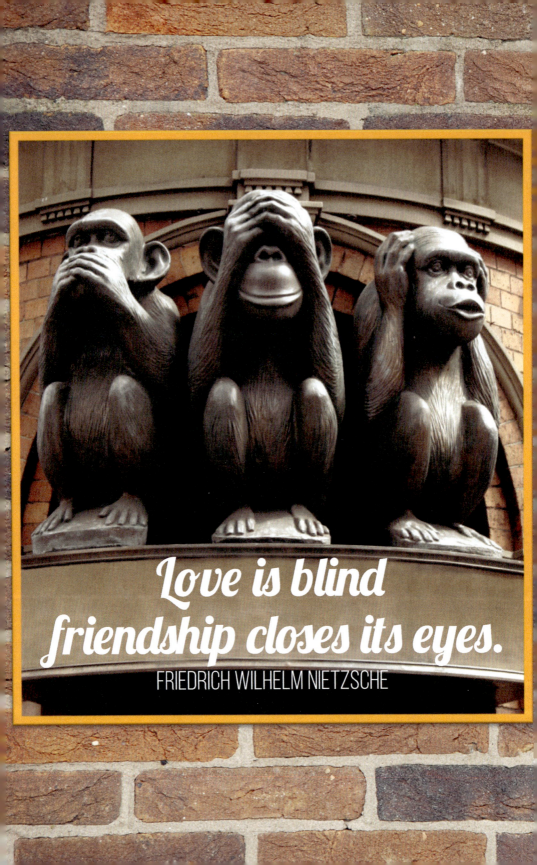

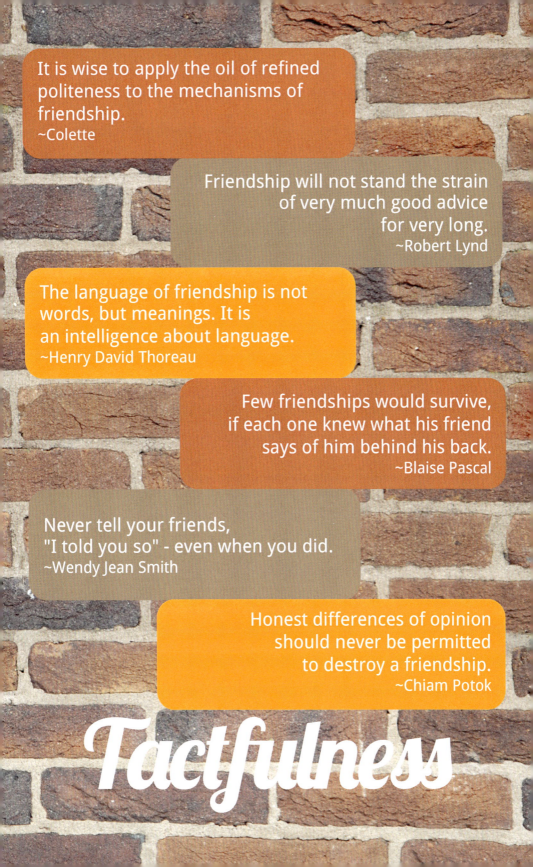

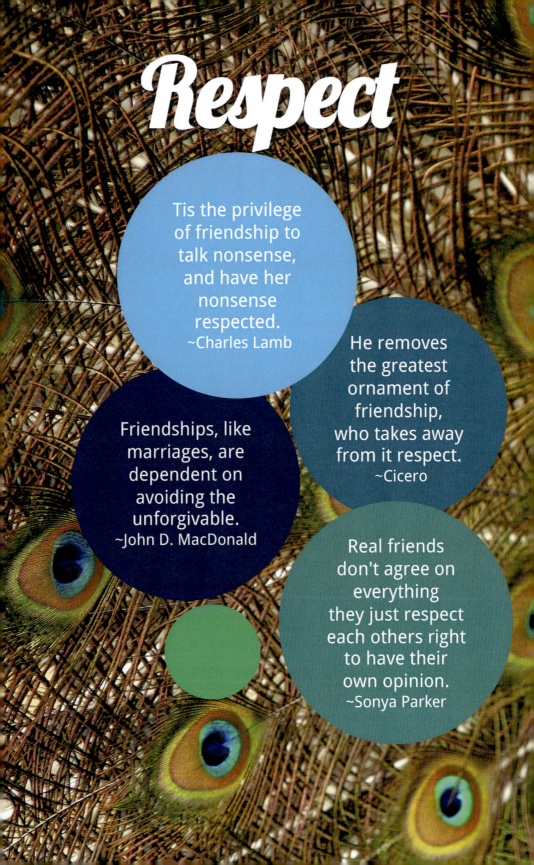

Shelter

Friendship is certainly the finest balm for the pangs of disappointed love.
~Jane Austen

When someone allows you to bear his burdens, you have found deep friendship.
~Real Live Preacher

It's the friends you can call up at 4 a.m.
~Marlene Dietrich

Friendship is a cozy shelter from life's rainy days
~Unknown

Friendship is like a sheltering tree.
~Samuel Taylor Coleridge

Adversity is the touchstone of friendship.
~French Proverb

Friendship

IS ONE OF THE
SWEETEST JOYS

of life. Many might have failed beneath the bitterness of their trial had they not found a friend.

CHARLES SPURGEON

Joy

> Friendship improves happiness and reduces misery, by doubting our joys and dividing our grief.
> ~Joseph Addison

> Only solitary men know the full joys of friendship. Others have their family; but to a solitary and an exile his friends are everything.
> ~Warren Gamaliel Harding

> And in the sweetness of friendship let there be laughter and the sharing of pleasures. For in the dew of little things the heart finds its morning and is refreshed.
> ~Kahlil Gibran

The worst solitude
is to be destitute
of sincere friendship.
~Sir Francis Bacon

Value

True friendship
is like sound health;
the value of it
is seldom known
until it be lost.
~Charles Caleb Colton

Friendship
is unnecessary,
like philosophy, like art...
It has no survival value;
rather it is one of those things
that give value to survival.
~C. S. Lewis

Personal Growth

Friendship is a strong and habitual inclination in two persons to promote the good and happiness of one another.
~Eustace Budgell

No person is your friend who demands your silence, or denies your right to grow.
~Alice Walker

My best friend is the one who brings out the best in me.
~Henry Ford

Altruism

There is no friendship in trade.
~Cornelius Vanderbilt

Friendship is selfless love, care, respect, and honor not a profitable opportunity.
~Santosh Kalwar

The finest kind of friendship is between people who expect a great deal of each other but never ask it.
~Sylvia Bremer

If we would build on a sure foundation in friendship, we must love friends for their sake rather than for our own.
~Charlotte Bronte

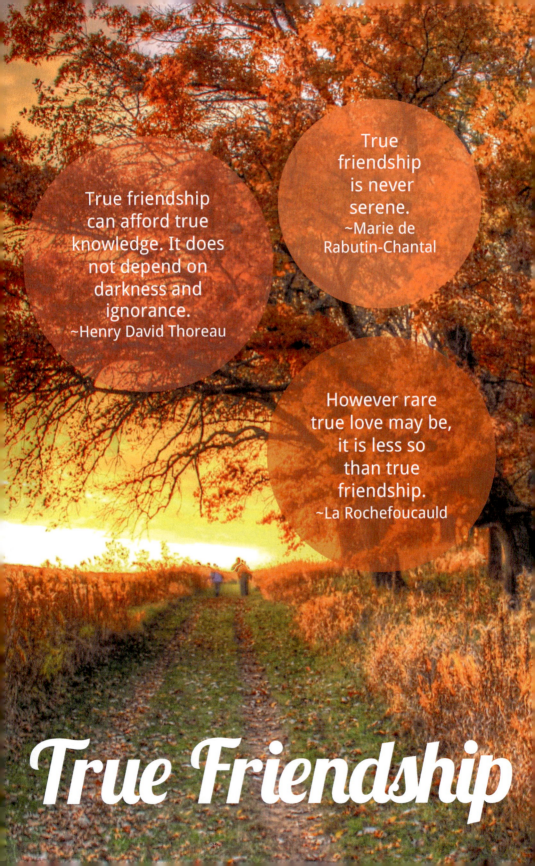

Preciousness

Friendships are fragile things and require as much handling as any other fragile and precious thing.
~Randolph Silliman Bourne

Real friendship, like real poetry, is extremely rare - and precious as a pearl.
~Tahar Ben Jelloun

Friendship multiplies the good in life and divides the evil.
~Baltasar Gracian

Friendship make prosperity more shining and lessens adversity by dividing and sharing it.
~Cicero

Friendship is **PRECIOUS** not only in the shade, but in the sunshine of life.

BALTASAR GRACIAN

Essence of Life

Of all the things which wisdom provides to make us entirely happy, much the greatest is the possession of friendship.
~Epicurus

The better part of one's life consists of his friendships.
~Abraham Lincoln

Friendship is the golden thread that ties the hearts of all hearts of all the world.
~John Evelyn

Friendship is the highest degree of perfection in society.
~Michel Eyquem de Montaigne

Friendship is neither a formality nor a mode it is rather a life.
~David Grayson

World

A friend is the one who comes in when the whole world has gone out.
~Grace Pulpit

Wherever we are it is our friends that make our world.
~Henry Drummond

Each friend represents a world in us, a world possibly not born until they arrive, and it is only by this meeting that a new world is born.
~Anaïs Nin

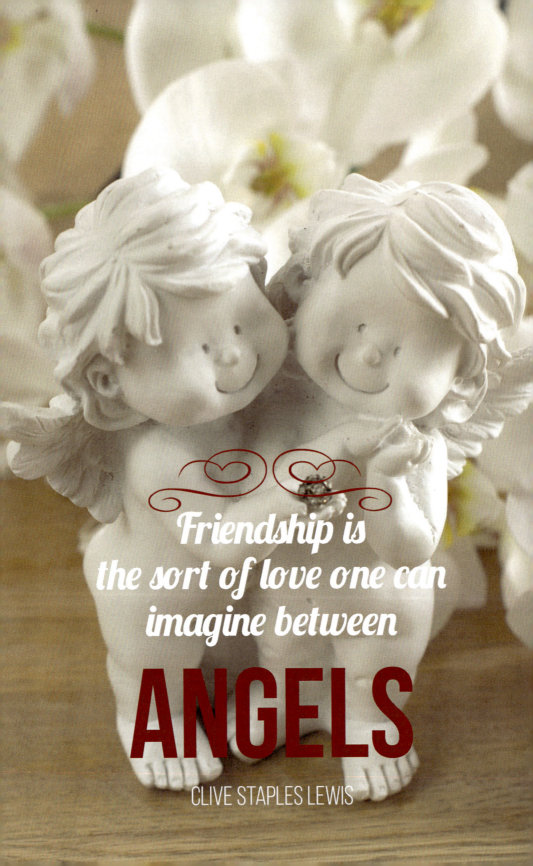

Love

Friendship is love with understanding.
~Unknown

Love comes from blindness, friendship from knowledge
~Comte DeBussy-Rabutin

Friendship often ends in love but love in friendship - never.
~Charles Caleb Colton

Love demands infinitely less than friendship.
~Ethel Watts Mumford

It is not a lack of love, but a lack of friendship that makes unhappy marriages.
~Friedrich Wilhelm Nietzsche

Money

The holy passion of friendship is of so sweet and steady and loyal and enduring a nature that it will last through a whole lifetime, if not asked to lend money.
~Mark Twain

It is a good thing to be rich, it is a good thing to be strong, but it is a better thing to be beloved of many friends.
~Euripides

Friendship is like money, easier made than kept.
~Samuel Butler

A friendship founded on business is better than a business founded on friendship.
~John D. Rockefeller Jr.

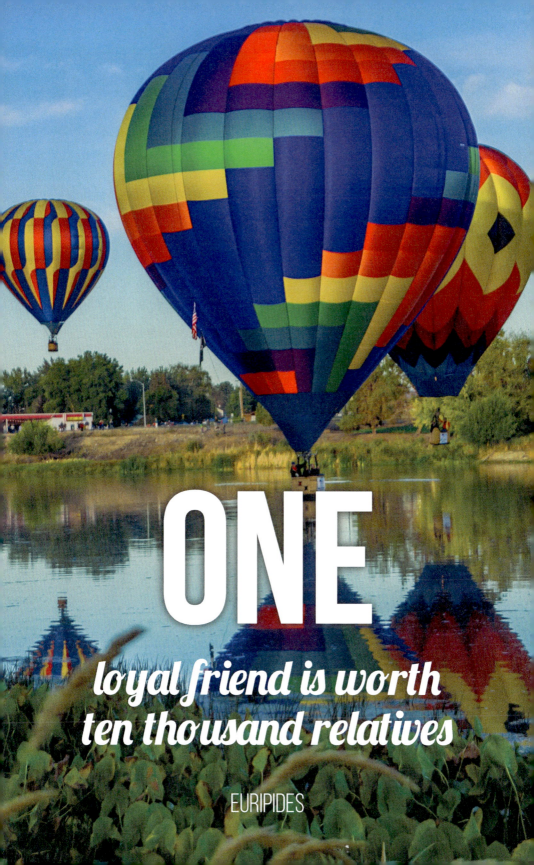

Stand the test of time

Those truly linked don't need correspondence, When they meet again after many years apart, their friendship is as true as ever.
~Deng Ming-Dao

Depth of friendship does not depend on length of acquaintance.
~Rabindranath Tagore

Friendships that have stood the test of time and change are surely best.
~Joseph Parry

The friendship that can cease has never been real.
~Saint Jerome

SUBSCRIBE TO MY NEWSLETTER!

Hello! What's your name? It's nice to meet you!
I'd love to send you each week
new inspirational quotes, easy healthy recipes
and also advanced tips to make healthy habits stick.
I'm very much looking forward to seeing
you there again. Until then I'm wishing you
all the best and enjoy!

SIGN UP TODAY

http://leanjumpstart.com/newsletter

OTHER TITLES YOU MIGHT LIKE:

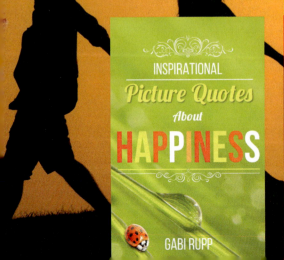

Gabi Rupp is a certified coach, author and entrepreneur. Prior to her work online, Gabi spent more than a decade as a marketing executive, mostly in the food and nutrition field, helping her clients realize their own projects. After her daughter was born, she found her true calling: writing, teaching, and coaching. Having the perfect life/work balance gave her the freedom to be a fulltime mother. In 2013 she founded www.leanjumpstart.com, where she uses a successful combination of proven science and practical experience to help people get in shape and stick with their new, healthy habits. Gabi is now happily settled in a little German town near the beautiful Black Forest region and spends her days with family, friends, and assisting clients as they overcome limitations and live life to its fullest potential.

Publisher: Gabi Rupp, www.Leanjumpstart.com / gabi@leanjumpstart.com
Concept, Design & Layout: Gabi Rupp
Photo Credits: Footage Firm Inc., Dollar Photo Club ©: adrenalinapura, aleksandr, kbuntu, mutai, rawpixel sumire8, Thorsten, UMC_Africatrip, zoomteam
1. Edition 2015

ISBN-13: 978-1508761945
ISBN-10: 1508761949
© Gabi Rupp

Made in the USA
Lexington, KY
20 November 2018